SELF-CARE

self-care

NEIL R. OLIVER

A **Self-Care** Guide
for **Psychological Calm,**
Emotional Stability, and
Physical Well-Being
in Times of Crisis.

ISBN (paperback): 978-0-6481113-6-8
ISBN (ebook): 978-0-6481113-7-5

Develop my intellect. Let me observe with clarity.

Your life will be whatever you choose it to be.

Be bold. Choose wisely.

Contents

Part 2: Psychological Self-Care

Part 3: Emotional Self-Care

Introduction

YOU MATTER. Your psychological state of being directly influences your emotional stability. Both impact your physical well-being and are responsible for the quality of your external and internal experiences. Implementing a healthy self-care regime in difficult times is essential. As you progress through this book you will discover many self-care strategies that you can apply in your life now that will increase the quality of your immediate experience.

Self-care is never more critical to our overall well-being than in times of crisis. Overall, this book is about establishing and maintaining good mental health by taking control of things you *can* control. It is light reading, although you may be exposed to some psychological practices which require you to consider and reflect upon. As you progress, many areas of self-care will be addressed across three main parts: Physical & Practical Self-Care, Psychological Self-Care, and Emotional Self-Care.

Ultimately this book has been designed to be what you need in your moment of need. You may choose to read from start to finish or go to the particular part of the book which meets your immediate needs. You may even want to pick and choose a chapter which is most relevant to you right now. No matter what approach you take, the contents within will have a significant impact on you psychologically, emotionally, physically, and practically. You will be stimulated. You will be provoked as you need to be, so you realise your power in living your best life right now despite whatever may be happening.

Keep a pen and highlighter near; make notes and study the content within these pages. Don't just read for the sake of finding a temporary escape from your problems. Master the content within so you can excel through this time in your life both psychologically calm and emotionally stable. As you equip yourself now, you are also protecting yourself from being vulnerable to the difficulties and challenges you may face in the future. Use this book as a reference over time to keep yourself in good mental health.

PART 1

Physical & Practical Self-Care

Physical Exercise

REGULAR EXERCISE IS great for your physical health, mental health, and immune system. Exercise is a remedy. Despite the temptations reducing your levels of motivation right now, you must move your body. The physical body is a powerful influencer of your psychological and emotional state of being. Being active each day will significantly increase your mental health and well-being by default.

If you are a person who regularly exercises, make sure you create a new routine as quickly as possible. As you do, you must let go of expectation. You will be tempted to indulge thoughts that attempt to prevent you from doing something positive for yourself because of your undesired internal experience. You must not look back and negatively compare what you're doing now to what you used to do before you were in crisis.

If you're not a regular exerciser, there really is no better time to start. Despite the temptation to give in to a lack of motivation, taking small steps to improve yourself will manifest more motivation within you. Don't complicate it; start small and keep it simple. If you're not sure what to do or how, jump online and do some research. There are many body weight training plans available which you can do in your own home. YouTube is another great resource for stay-at-home exercise options, too.

More than ever, you must be adaptable. We have to allow ourselves to be vulnerable to change when life isn't meeting our expectations. The best way through hard times is to control what we can. You can control moving your body, being active, and having an exercise plan. Having a regular exercise routine will provide you some additional benefits. You will have at least one thing to do each day. In addition, while you exercise you use up time without even realising it. Participating in exercise each day will help your perception of time to pass more quickly.

> "The best way through hard times
> is to control what we can.

Keep in mind that right now exercising is not about losing weight or trying to increase physical appearance. It's about maintaining good mental health and well-being. Use exercise as a remedy. Let it be a form of personal therapy which provides you psychological clarity as you navigate your way through such an uncertain time. One of the advantages of exercising that many people often overlook is the power of physical movement over psychological and emotional experience. As we move

our body purposefully, there is a whole range of biological processes taking place within our system that stimulates all kinds of
beneficial chemical reactions which directly impact our mental
health.

If you notice a change in your emotions, start moving your body.
If you start having negative thoughts, exercise. If fear is over-
whelming you, get active. Take control of what you can control. Your body is yours to control. This one decision to have
an exercise plan and follow through with it, regardless of what
is happening to you and around you, will be one of your best
decisions. Create a plan and execute your plan daily.

Nutrition

WHAT YOU PUT inside your body has a direct influence over your psychological state of mind and your emotional experience. Anything you ingest stimulates you. At a minimum, there will be a spike in your blood sugar levels. Blood sugar levels are a powerful influencer of emotion. In uncertain times, there will be the temptation to eat yourself through. Boredom alone can have you eating just for something to do with the additional benefit of giving you a temporary form of enjoyment.

It is important for your own mental well-being that you maintain proper balance. What you eat to nourish and fuel yourself through this time directly influences your thinking and emotions. You may not have considered food to be a stimulator of thought and emotion before. It is. And it's a powerful one. No one is suggesting you have to go on a strict meal plan right now or eat healthy foods only. Simply, at a minimum, you must be aware that what you put in your mouth does play a role in your mental health and then choose wisely.

In time of crisis you must eat well. If you haven't been eating as much due to fear, worry, doubt, and uncertainty, you must get back into a regular dietary routine. If you've noticed yourself overeating, stop. Both not eating regularly and overeating will directly impact your thought processes and the emotions you experience. Your body needs to be cared for through this time. How you treat it very much determines your quality of life right now. While there is so much uncertainty at the moment, and when many things are happening beyond your control, what you decide to eat, and how you choose to nourish your body, are decisions which are fully within your control. Take responsibility for controlling what you can.

"Take responsibility for controlling what you can.

As you navigate your way through this time, you will be tempted to eat for comfort. You may be doing it already. You may be doing it and haven't realised that you are doing it. We all need a way to find comfort. Your brain gravitates naturally toward pleasure and will try to obtain it through any means possible. As soon as we are gripped with uncertainty, we will need a way to pacify ourselves. There's no better, quicker, seemingly safer way to pacify ourselves than food. After all, it's not like we're taking drugs or drinking alcohol excessively, right?

Well, everything you eat directly impacts what you feel. How much you eat also has an impact. If you load your body up with more food than it needs, your system will work harder than it needs to in order to process, distribute, and eliminate what it has been given. This takes energy. Too much of anything is not a good idea. If you overload your system with excess, you will process longer and harder. More than you need will be distributed throughout your body, and the natural processes of elimination your body undertakes will be strained. All of this directly impacts your mental state of being and emotional experience.

Get back to the basics. As best as you can, try to nourish yourself with clean natural wholefoods; plenty of fruits and vegetables are essential. Ensure you are providing your body the adequate proteins, carbohydrates, and healthy fats your system needs to function well. The cleaner you eat, the better your mental health will be. Try to avoid the overconsumption of any kind of negative stimulants such as sugar and alcohol. Both can lead to weight gain, and they both impact your mental health in undesired ways.

It may also be a good idea for you to research your daily caloric intake requirements. Knowing how much fuel your body needs can help you keep track. When you do the research, it may surprise you to find you are eating more than your body needs.

Making some simple adjustments to what you're eating, and how much you're consuming, can take a lot of pressure off your body that is directly impacting your mental health.

Sleep

SLEEP IS ANOTHER critically important component of good mental health and general well-being. It's important that sleep is given the attention it deserves. As you endure all the challenges associated with experiencing a time of crisis, being able to function at your best will be of advantage to you. There will be an increased demand on you to make decisions and take the most appropriate action as you navigate yourself through this hard time. If you're not in a good psychological state, the quality of your decision-making will be affected. With a negatively impaired psychological state, what you will or won't do will become based on the quality of your emotional experience in the present moment rather than coming from a place of calm, rational judgement due to sound mental health. Without the right balance of sleep, your ability to function well mentally will be impaired.

With more time on your hands, having to stay home, and being restricted in your ability to venture outdoors, you may well be tempted to sleep in a little more than normal. While there is nothing wrong with a sleep-in every now and again, be careful to not allow yourself to overindulge in sleep-ins every day. Getting up and getting active, despite your circumstances, will help you keep your levels of motivation high. Staying in bed gives you time to indulge negative thought patterns such as, *What am I going to do today? What's the point in getting up? I'm so over this, when will it change?* etc. Negative thought patterns can lead to depression. It's essential you do what you can to minimise the risk of any unwanted psychological and emotional experiences as a result of this difficult time in your life.

" Negative thought patterns can lead to depression. It's essential you do what you can to minimise the risk of any unwanted psychological and emotional experiences as a result of this difficult time in your life.

Because you have more challenges to deal with on top of your normal responsibilities when compared to your pre-crisis routine, you may be tempted to stay up a little later than normal because your mind is so pre-occupied with overthinking. You may even find yourself staying up into the early hours of the morning. Every once in a while, this is okay. But if you keep doing this, you will disrupt your sleeping patterns which can directly impact your psychological and emotional well-being. Both sleeping in and staying up late can lead to patterns of overthinking. Lying in bed just because you can may lead the mind to wander. Staying up late gives the mind more time than it should to entertain the fear and uncertainty you are experiencing.

Sleep gives your physical body time to recover, recharge, and restore. The same is true psychologically and emotionally. Sleep is a time for your mental processes to rest. One of the best ways to escape the dilemmas and problems you face is to sleep them away. It's hard to consciously stress about something if you're not conscious in the first place. While I'm not suggesting using sleep as an exclusive way to escape your problems, it must be an essential part of your coping strategies throughout this time to ensure you remain mentally sound.

As best as you can, keep your sleeping pattern as normal as it can be. Have a sleep-in every now and again. Don't feel guilty if you stay up late every now and again; just make sure you strike a balance. Keep in mind that when you are awake, your conscious experience is impacted by the duration and quality of your sleep the night before. Make the effort to set a routine for yourself which keeps you functioning at your highest potential. Sleep is another thing you can control right now while everything else in your life may seem to be out of control.

Grooming

MAINTAINING DISCIPLINE WITH your grooming routine is critical. Grooming is often ignored as a powerful influencer over a person's general well-being. You will benefit greatly If you force yourself to maintain good grooming habits despite the challenges and difficulties you are facing. Keeping up a good grooming routine increases confidence; it impacts self-worth and helps motivate. Simple things such as taking a long hot shower and making the effort to dress well, even though you don't really have anywhere to go, provide a significant boost to mental health.

Good personal grooming standards help keep you in a regular routine. Despite all the uncertainty you're facing, it is important that you maintain some form of normality in your life. Ensuring you keep your normal grooming routine helps in this way. Make the effort to get up, get showered, and dress nicely each day. Don't just lounge around because you can't take the initiative to look after yourself. Brush your teeth. Maybe you have nowhere to go but do your hair nicely anyway. Do you want to catch a reflection of yourself in a mirror looking scruffy and unkept, or would you rather see yourself looking well?

You can also use showering as a tool to increase your well-being. Anytime you notice yourself starting to feel a bit down, have a nice hot shower. If you find yourself overwhelmed with over-thinking, take a shower. If fear, doubt, worry, and uncertainty are bombarding you, take a shower. Warm water is a boost. The simple act of taking a shower can have a massive impact on you, even if it's for no other reason than to break the repetitious patterns of disempowering psychological processes. Have you ever noticed that you always feel good after swimming? Taking a shower can provide the same result.

It's important in times of crisis that we take the time to do what we can to boost our confidence. Simply dressing well and doing our hair has a huge impact on our perception of ourselves. Often this perception is formed subconsciously beyond our own conscious awareness. As you endure through the uncertainty of this crisis, anything you can do to boost your confidence while you are tempted to entertain fear and uncertainty will be of advantage to you. Don't drop your personal grooming standards just because your normal daily responsibilities have diminished.

It's important in times of crisis that we take the time to do what we can to boost our confidence.

You don't want to be in a situation where many aspects of your life all compound out of control because of one larger influence.

Yes, you may be facing pressures now you never expected. You may be gripped with fear and overrun with uncertainty; but that does not mean you have to let other areas of your life diminish as well. Minimise the impact on yourself personally by controlling what you can. You are in total control over personal grooming. Make the effort. Your physical appearance directly impacts your thoughts and emotions. Maintaining a good grooming routine is another simple way you can maintain sound mental health.

"You don't want to be in a situation where many aspects of your life all compound out of control because of one larger influence.

Create a Routine

KEEPING A REGULAR routine is critically important to maintaining good mental health. Having a routine can keep you from becoming disempowered, demotivated, and helpless. Having things to do each day gives you purpose. Having a routine provides you some form of normality. In having a routine, you are able to cater to two of your most important psychological needs: significance and certainty. Having a routine gives you purpose, executing and completing your routine makes you feel productive, and being productive reinforces your own personal sense of worth. Knowing you have a routine to follow through with also allows you to structure your life with a little certainty. When I get up tomorrow, I know I'm going to do this, this, and this. By default, having a plan makes you feel good and keeps you occupied from entertaining some other negative disempowering things which you could entertain if you weren't keeping busy.

You may not have previously realised the importance of routine until it was taken from you. Often, we don't realise the significance of many things until they change, or we lose them altogether. We are very much creatures of habit. Having a regular routine gives us a sense of certainty. As much as you may have hated getting up and having to go to work, or getting the kids ready in the morning, these undesired tasks do provide for us in many ways we aren't aware of psychologically. Simple things like getting up, getting organised, and getting on with the day are rarely credited to be of importance. However, they have a huge impact on your state of mind and emotional well-being.

It is important to manifest as much certainty as possible in uncertain times. Controlling what we can gives us back a sense of power and control over our lives. Our perception is very quickly influenced by our immediate experience. The more we entertain fear and uncertainty, the sooner we will start to believe we are powerless. The truth is that you are the one who holds all the authority, power, and control over what is happening within your internal experience right now in the present moment. If you execute your authority and put your power into controlling what is yours to control, you can navigate your way through uncertain times masterfully.

"It is important to manifest as much certainty as possible in uncertain times.

Use your ability to plan and then execute a regular routine as a form of distraction. If you keep yourself busy, occupied with tasks and other things, you have less time to indulge in fear, uncertainty, overthinking or any other form of negative psychological influence. Your routine can provide you a powerful psychological escape which requires no real conscious mental effort on your part. Use your routine as a distraction which gives you purpose. Keeping busy can be your remedy. Keep your routine regular and be consistent with it. It can take between 21 and 67 days to form new habitual behaviours. The sooner you get yourself going the sooner you can recreate a sense of normality in your life which caters to your psychological need for certainly.

Plan Your Week

BE PURPOSEFUL IN forming a new routine. Take the time in advance to sit yourself down and strategically think about what you would like to achieve over the coming week. Make a list of every possibility; it can be narrowed down later. Determining your routine in advance by planning the week ahead can make you feel as if you have power and control over some part of your life once again. Rather than reacting to everything that is happening to you and around you, take the time to be purposeful in preparing yourself to go in a direction of your own choosing in the upcoming week.

> *Be purposeful in forming a new routine.*

Be determined that each week you will make the decision to take time out to plan the week ahead. Knowing what you're going to do and why will give you a plan; it will provide you with a sense of purpose. Your willingness to occupy yourself with goals, to do's, and things you desire to achieve each week will play a significant role in maintaining good mental health. Just because you are making a plan doesn't mean you have to accomplish everything you wanted to achieve over the week. There must be a degree of adaptability and flexibility as you progress through the week you have planned.

Being adaptable and flexible in your approach allows you to move on and change course without indulging in consequences of unmet expectations and things not turning out as you expected them to. You don't want anything else to influence your current state of being in a negative way. So adapt, be flexible, and keep moving forward free from negative distractions. It is very likely that you have more time right now than ever to do whatever you want to do. So, if you make a list and don't achieve it all as planned, add whatever you didn't get done this week to next week's list.

Keep your plan for the week simple. It may not be a good idea to cram twenty things onto your list for the week. You're already under enough pressure right now, dealing with all the uncertainty surrounding what might happen. Design your plan for the week to be achievable and fun. The whole idea of having a plan for the week is to give you certainty and purpose, while increasing your general confidence by achieving what you wanted to accomplish. Figure out what it might take and what you might want to achieve, so you can then define the upcoming week as a good one.

" *Keep your plan for the week simple.*

Be sure to add in plenty of fun, enjoyable tasks into your plan for the week. Maybe Friday night will be movie night. Maybe Wednesday morning you might decide to have a hot cooked breakfast. Saturday lunch might be a BBQ. Plan things you enjoy, and whatever they may be, look forward to them, and use them to create a sense of excitement for the week. This strategy really does have an impact on your mental health. Having things to look forward to brightens your perspective and perception. Having nothing to look forward to causes you to lose hope and indulge in misery. Also, try to diversify the activities in your plan into categories such as work, exercise, recreation time, fun, educational, social, family, etc. Having a range of things to do over many different areas will keep your brain engaged. Be flexible, change your plan as and when you need to, adapt to whatever comes your way, and be flexible enough to make a diversion if your plans seem to change.

Plan Your Day

HAVING A ROUTINE and planning your week doesn't necessarily mean you have a plan for the day. It is important that each day you re-evaluate whatever is on your plan and adapt it to suit yourself in the present moment. As you navigate yourself through all the challenges arising in your time of crisis, you must keep yourself flexible. After all, you're the one who has the authority to execute power and control in your life. You want to be flexible enough to change your plans if you so desire. If you wake up and decide you'd prefer to do something else, do it. The point of having a routine and developing a plan for the week was to give you purpose and direction. There is nothing to say you can't change your plan as you desire.

Every day re-evaluate your plan and adjust it to suit yourself. Moment by moment, your state of mind will be influenced by what is happening around you and what is happening to you. Observe what you are experiencing and change course to suit yourself. Set each day up to be as interesting and fun as it can be. Let fun and good emotional experiences be the goal you set out to achieve each day. Don't let them be the only goal, but make sure they are included in your daily routine. If your mind perceives you have something to look forward to, you will experience the psychological and emotional benefit in advance of what you are looking forward to before you even participate in it.

" *Let fun and good emotional experiences be the goal you set out to achieve each day.*

Each day try to wake up and get going as quickly as you can. This will increase your levels of motivation. Once you have taken time to wake, groom, and have breakfast, it's then time to create momentum. Try to tick something off your list of daily tasks as early in the day as you can. This will create a sense of achievement which will then motivate you to participate in the rest of the tasks you identified at the beginning of the day. Getting things done satisfies. I should mention also that your routine, weekly plan, and daily plan do not have to include things that need to be done. Your list may include reading a chapter of a book, watching an episode of your favourite TV program, or jumping online and researching something you've always wanted to learn. Don't make a plan that consists only of getting things done around the house.

Don't overload yourself with too many tasks for the day. Again, keep things simple and adapt to your day as you see fit. Take all the pressure off yourself. Your plan is not about getting things done and making sure you achieve; it is about maintaining a good balance of psychological and emotional well-being by providing yourself with direction and purpose while maintaining a sense of fun. Achieving the emotional experiences you desire should be at the forefront of your thinking each day. Enjoy being the captain of your own ship while you can. Eventually this crisis will pass, and life will get back to some form of normality. That normality may not include as much freedom as you have to be your own captain right now.

One last objective you should set out to achieve each day is to reward yourself for successfully completing your daily plan. It is important to have things to look forward to. Knowing there is a reward at the end of the day can motivate you to do what needs to be done. And the great thing about setting up this reward system for yourself is that you can cheekily still give yourself the reward even if you don't do everything on your list. Have fun! You're your own captain, remember?

Keep Busy

HAVING A ROUTINE, planning your week, and planning each day allow you to be purposeful in creating new behaviours as quickly as possible which, in return, cater to your psychological needs. Good mental health requires your psychological needs to be met as you need them met in the healthiest way possible. Keeping yourself busy is a healthy way to meet your needs as you need them met without even realising the benefit you are receiving psychologically within your conscious awareness.

One of the payoffs in keeping yourself busy is it distracts you. As you proceed to get things done and occupy yourself with tasks each day, you are distracting yourself from having to indulge, entertain, and participate in the negative, undesired thought processes which accompany fear and uncertainty. Fear and uncertainty very quickly manifest panic and anxiety. By keeping yourself busy and having things to do and look forward to, you are challenging your intellectual focus in a more productive way which ultimately benefits you.

Ignorance is equally your best friend and worst enemy. Throughout this time, use your ability to ignore fear and uncertainty by channelling your focus into the productive tasks you've planned for the day. Using ignorance to your advantage, keeping busy is a great form of distraction which can provide you an escape from the psychological torment and emotional trauma you will endure if you were to entertain fear and uncertainty. While using busyness as a distraction and escape is not a permanent solution to your problems, they can be the perfect tonic you can use to get yourself through another day.

The busier you keep yourself, the more you are likely to accomplish. Achievement can provide you will a sense of fulfilment. Completing tasks reinforces your worth with the additional upside of being productive. You can achieve a lot if you plan ahead. You can delight yourself in accomplishment and indulge in rewarding yourself if you execute your plan. A time of crisis does not define who you are or what you're capable of. *You* do. How you react, the decisions you make, and the actions you take are all within your control right now.

" A time of crisis does not define who you are or what you're capable of. How you react, the decisions you make, and the actions you take are all within your control right now.

There may be many external factors beyond your control right now, but you are far from powerless. Every task you complete in the present moment reinforces your own personal sense of power and control. You are anything but powerless right now. You don't have to live your life feeling helpless. Keep active, remain busy for good portions of your day, and the consequences of negative thoughts and emotions will not torment and traumatise you. As you keep yourself busy, you will have less time to worry about future events.

Strategically try to distract yourself, and time will pass quickly. The more your head is focused on something productive, the less you will be aware of the time, or even what day it is. In keeping busy you will lose your perception of time, and days will pass quicker than you realise. In no time, the week will have passed, and you'll be planning the next. Don't underestimate your influence. If you keep active and occupy yourself with things to do, you will naturally inspire those around you. In a time of crisis, people need someone to look up to, someone to lead the way, someone they can follow. Be that for someone else. Let your actions inspire the people in your life positively. A positive attitude is infectious (in a good way).

Avoid Negative Influences

IT IS CRITICAL to your mental health that you minimise your exposure to news programs, newspapers, and social media. Generally, these methods of delivering information and supposedly informing the public are overwhelmingly negative, having a huge impact on your mental health whether you realise it or not. Constant exposure to news sources and social media will saturate your thinking both consciously and subconsciously. You can soon be influenced negatively without any conscious awareness.

While it is important to stay informed and keep up-to-date with the latest information, especially relating to your health and health protocols, you need to stay informed yet minimise your exposure. You can't be watching the news every hour and expecting you will cope psychologically. You can't keep checking social media every ten minutes and expect to maintain a good state of emotion. It might be best to limit your exposure to news programs and social media to morning and night. Anything more will affect your mental well-being.

I would even suggest you strategically plan to ignore all news programming and avoid social media for two or three days at a time every week or so to ensure you maintain good psychological and emotional balance. There's no real downside to avoiding negative influences in your life. Ultimately, what you watch and how you feed your focus stimulates you. You are in control of what stimulates you psychologically. Don't let anything beyond your control have the power or authority to influence your emotions in a negative way.

" It is critical to your mental health that you minimise your exposure to news programs, newspapers, and social media.

Part of many people's daily routine is to check up on recent news events. You may want to re-evaluate your plan for each day and make some decisions around what and who you allow to have influence over you. Media of all forms are constantly bombarding our intellect with fear, worry, doubt, and uncertainty. Much of the time it happens subconsciously; we simply aren't aware of it. You can be deceived into experiencing all sorts of undesired internal experiences before you ever become consciously aware you've been influenced. Be diligent in maintaining a good state of observation over what is influencing you and how.

In addition to news programming and social media, people can also be an unintentional form of negative influence. Being around people right now who are constantly complaining about how bad their life is, constantly expressing their fears and worries about the future, will have a negative effect on you. All of a sudden, if you're not careful. You can find yourself entertaining the same types of thinking and emotions as those people around you. The more you value a person, the more potential there is for them to have influence over you because you care about them. Address anyone who may be bringing you down because of their own problems. Be very careful to create an environment for yourself which is uplifting. Ensure those people around you do their best to build you up, and make sure you do the same.

If, all of a sudden, you find yourself for feeling unusually negative, down, or thinking poorly for no good reason, leaving you experiencing undesired emotions, re-evaluate what you're allowing to influence your intellectual focus. Very often you will find it's the influence of news programming, social media, or the people closest to you which are having a real impact on the quality of your internal psychological and emotional well-being.

Get Outdoors

EXPOSING YOURSELF TO the elements of nature can impact you significantly. Breathing fresh air, feeling the sun on your face, and just being exposed to something other than the confines of your own home, all help to maintain good mental health. If you are unable to leave your home, you can still open a window or door and spend some time looking out. Even looking out an open window and feeling the wind circulating around your body can help change your focus. In hard times we have an opportunity to reflect on what's really important. Exposing yourself to the outdoors is the perfect way to rekindle your appreciation for the little things, such as sunlight, fresh air, trees, flowers, etc.

It is ideal to get outdoors each and every day for at least thirty minutes. Add going outside into your daily plan. You don't have to venture far. Even standing in your yard will do. You don't have to leave home. You will be tempted to ignore getting outside, mostly because you may not have realised how much of an impact being outside has on your psychological well-being and emotional stability. You must observe yourself closely through this time. Before you know it, three days could have passed with you locked up inside and suffering psychologically as a result.

With our capacity to function normally being stripped from us during this time, we must take advantage of the freedoms we do have. Getting outdoors is freedom within your control. If you have the freedom to get outside, you must not stay locked up. Those people who stay indoors for prolonged periods are increasing their risk of anxiety and depression. If exercise is an allowable activity where you live, make the effort to complete your daily exercise routine outdoors as much as you can.

" With our capacity to function normally being stripped from us during this time, we must take advantage of the freedoms we do have.

As you expose yourself to the outdoors, consider taking the time to be grateful. Experiencing gratitude in the present moment is a very powerful strategy you can use to change your general well-being. Gratitude helps shift our focus. Each time we shift our focus in a positive direction, we always experience the positive emotions generated by positive thought processes. Shifting your focus so you can experience gratitude is not complicated. All you need to do is make the effort to pay attention to things you usually ignore in your daily life; notice them, appreciate them, be grateful for them.

You might notice the sounds of birds chirping. Maybe you marvel at their ability to fly effortlessly through the air. Maybe the morning dew on the grass and how it sparkles in the sunlight catches your attention. Take the time to smell those nice flowers in the garden. There is no limit to the number of things in your life right now that you can focus on positively and be grateful for. Ignorance is both your best friend and your worst enemy. Ignore your problems by directing your focus onto something else for which you can show gratitude.

Ultimately, getting outdoors brings back a level of vitality that being indoors cannot produce in you. Taking time to get out will revitalise your mind and emotions. Being outdoors will make you feel good for no apparent reason other than being outside. If you are stuck in a rut with your thinking: get outside. If your emotions are negative, or if you start feeling sad: get up and get outdoors. Even five minutes outside can help you regain perspective.

Enjoy the Small Things

YOU MAY NOT have realised this, but the simple things in life are often some of the best. We tend to lead busy complex lives, often overlooking the little things in favour of our ambitions and determined dedication to achieving our goals. When times are hard, it is important to take the time to step back and search for those things in life that are simple yet satisfying. What are some simple things that provide you pleasure? Just by asking yourself this question, you're asking your brain to find an answer. You may be surprised with the response.

Is it reading your favourite book that brings you pleasure? Is it that first cup of coffee you have in the morning? Taking time to watch a movie? What is it for you? For me, I created a very simple way to manifest gratitude in my own life by challenging my focus onto something small which brings me great joy. It is simply knowing that I have a few dollars in my pocket to go down to my favourite café a buy a nice coffee. You have to set yourself up to win so you don't buy into the doom and gloom which can tempt you to spiral out of control.

Of course, most of us all have bigger things for which we can be grateful. But stripping things back to their simplest form, and being grateful for them without the complexity associated with our normal daily life, is really therapeutic. Your appreciation for the little things will shift your focus and allow you to benefit psychologically. When your conscious awareness is channelled into something small, it engenders gratitude in the present moment and stimulates a positive emotional response.

Let gratitude for the small things provide the psychological remedy you need. Renew your appreciation for the simple pleasures found in your life. In addition to being grateful for the small things in your life, what are the little things you can use to stimulate a sense of excitement in your life right now? What little things can you use or create as a reward to excite you during this time? How can you use them to get excited? What can you use to look forward to which will manifest excitement within you right now?

Take some time to reflect on these questions. Make the effort to set yourself up to win. The quality of your emotions is heavily influenced by you and what you choose to focus upon. You are the authority who has power and control over your own internal experience. Take responsibility for controlling what you can. It is easy to direct your focus onto something which is to your advantage. Renew your appreciation, allow yourself to be excited, and give yourself permission to be excited about the little things. Be kind to yourself. Reward yourself.

"You are the authority who has power and control over your own internal experience.

You may even decide to maintain your newfound appreciation for the small pleasures of life post crisis. After all, having something positive to focus on can only benefit you. Being able to shift your focus so you benefit psychologically and emotionally is a strategy you can apply as your daily life progresses back to normal. In this way, you can avoid some of the stress associated with the pressure of your daily responsibilities.

Have Something to Look Forward To

YOU MUST FIND ways to set yourself up to win as you endure through this time of crisis and progress through the varying stages of post-crisis life. There are already so many things in your life which are beyond your control already. Everything beyond your control has the power to influence you negatively. Before you know it, you can find yourself unhappy, with your mind quickly spiralling out of control. Defining new rules in your life can have a huge impact on your mental well-being. It allows you to perceive that you are winning even in small ways. And this is fully within your control.

As you navigate through this crisis, one of the best things you can desire right now is the right kind of good emotions. Put your mind to work creating the quality of emotions which are most beneficial to you as your progress forward. This will be a huge advantage for you.

After all, is it not true that the quality of your life really is defined by the quality of your psychological state and emotional experience moment by moment?

Set yourself up to experience fun, excitement, joy, and fulfilment right here, right now. There's no point living life waiting until we get what we want, or having our expectations met, before we will allow ourselves to experience fun, excitement, joy, and fulfilment. Since there is so much uncertainty in your life right now, how long will it be until you are satisfied that you are getting what you want? When will your expectations be met?

" Use every strategy you can to keep your focus away from negative thought patterns as you endure each day.

One of the easiest ways to create fun, build excitement, achieve joy, and experience fulfilment is to have something achievable to look forward to today, this week, and this month. If you take time to shift your focus onto the small things that you can be grateful for, you're already on your way. If you use choose to look forward to these small things that bring you simple pleasure, you are setting yourself up to experience good emotions in the future.

The concept of using rewards as you complete daily and weekly tasks is a useful and fun way to build excitement. Completing your tasks allows you to achieve joy, especially if you reward yourself for achieving them. Creating a reward system allows you to look forward in a positive way. This is so important when there will naturally be some many negative future-based emotions that attempt to steal your focus through this time.

Rewards are an important psychological tool which you must not overlook. Looking forward to something by default stimulates positive psychological processes. Having something to look forward to allows you to experience a better quality of emotional experience in the present moment. Good emotional experience is priceless. Having pleasurable things to look forward to will help you maintain a positive perspective in a difficult time.

Incentivise your day and week. Use rewards to keep yourself on track and in good spirits. If you want to create an internal state of being that is optimistic, ensure you are looking forward to something today and in the week ahead. Keep it simple. Use every strategy you can to keep your focus away from negative thought patterns as you endure each day.

Be a Little Indulgent

THERE'S NO RIGHT or wrong way to endure through a crisis. Sometimes it's just a matter of surviving the best we can right here, right now, and being okay with it. We have to accept there will be times when our thoughts get the better of us. Our emotions will sour at times. There may be times where you're not motivated to do positive things for yourself in order to change your focus. So, what then?

// *There's no right or wrong way to endure through a crisis.*

How about self-medicating in the form of indulgence? Let me be clear. I am not an ambassador for you to abandon all sense and let yourself go crazy in indulging everything and anything you want in the quantities you want them. I am suggesting to you that it is okay to participate in indulging yourself in something in your moment of need if you're struggling to cope temporarily. The intention is not to become dependent on using external vehicles to survive; but there may be a time when getting through right now requires chocolate. Maybe you need the glass of wine to stay sane right now. If you need to eat your feelings using ice cream: go for it. If you want to waste a day binge watching TV: do it.

Whatever it takes when you are at your lowest point: do it. If indulging in ice-cream is what you need to survive: go for it. Drink the wine without feeling guilty. Indulge in whatever you need to in order to release the psychological pressure and achieve a shift in your emotions. As you proceed though each day, don't think twice about using an indulgence as a temporary form of therapy. Just make sure that whatever you have chosen to indulge in is not used every day. Normally, if a person was to receive conventional psychological therapy, they would see their therapist once or twice a week. Let this be your guide. Over-indulging once or twice a week is acceptable, but every day is not. If you do indulge every day, you run the risk of using your indulgence in a way that ultimately becomes self-destructive by having a negative impact on your psychological well-being.

Don't fear being indulgent. Be careful not to associate any negative meaning to being temporarily indulgent in order to cope. It doesn't have to mean anything more than you made a decision to do what needed to be done in order to cope through today. It's okay. Give yourself permission to let go every once in a while. Don't go crazy with it, but be okay with it. Sometimes a little indulgence is just what's needed to escape the boredom of being locked up inside and unable to live your normal life.

Moderation is key here. Sometimes indulgences are necessary to survive; but be aware that overindulgences will not have you thrive if you participate in them regularly. Indulgence really is a healthy form of escape when used in moderation. Don't worry about how others may judge you. Do what you need to do in order to survive your worst moments well. There's no shame in it. Don't give in to the temptation to feel guilty. Guilt won't serve you well. That chocolate will. That ice-cream surely will. That glass of wine will. Escaping through binge- watching TV will. Give yourself permission. It's okay.

Set Some Achievable Goals

BEING IN CRISIS and not being able to participate in your normal activities does provide you with a useful opportunity to reflect and re-evaluate your life. Sometimes a crisis is the only occasion when we will take time to reflect on our lives and think about the direction we are headed. This time can be an opportunity for you to indulge in the idea of other possibilities for your life. If you accept the opportunity, you have right now to re-evaluate what you want in life. You can then put in motion the necessary steps to birth your newly perceived possibility into reality.

Being in a crisis does not mean you can't improve yourself in some way. You have a tremendous opportunity to take time right now to develop yourself and your skill set in meaningful ways. Do you have time to read, time to study, or can you complete an online course? Maybe you've always wanted to write a book. Is now the perfect time? Any steps you take right now to improve yourself and your skill set will surely benefit you on the other side of this crisis. What can you do right now? What should you do? How can you position yourself in the best possible way now, so you're better equipped for your future?

Be determined to flourish and thrive despite the current situation you are in. What do you need to achieve right now, psychically, psychologically, and emotionally, that will benefit you? What goals do you need to achieve in order to prepare yourself for the future? What would be the most advantageous thing you can learn right now in preparation for your future? Take time to reflect. Answer these questions as quickly as you can. And then get to work.

" Being in a crisis does not mean you can't improve yourself in some way.

Your mental health will benefit tremendously by setting yourself up with some newly achievable goals right now. Your new goals will keep you focused in the present moment and on the future in a positive, constructive, empowering way. If you see this time as an opportunity to take advantage of, and take action in, executing this time to your advantage, you won't have as much time to entertain unwanted psychological patterns of thinking that lead to anxiety and depression.

When you figure out what you would like to achieve, you must take action. Put your intention into action immediately. It's important to allow your goal to be put into motion so it can gain immediate momentum. What are the first steps you need to execute to bring this possibility into reality? Do you need to research? Maybe you need to make a call or enquiry via a website. Maybe you need to make an appointment. Whatever it is, make sure you take action straight away.

If you take the time to set new goals and work toward them while enduring your crisis, the psychological advantage you will have in the future, knowing you took steps to improve yourself while in crisis, will bring about a tremendous sense of pride and fulfilment. It shows great character and real strength to know what steps to take in a crisis and then executing them. Decide to come out the other side better in at least one compartment of your life. And don't try to achieve everything right away. Enjoy the process.

Upskill Yourself

SETTING NEW GOALS is important. Setting goals keeps you motivated and moving forward in positive ways. Achieving goals brings about a tremendous sense of accomplishment and reinforces your worth. No matter what goals you hope to achieve, your goals must also be directed in upskilling you. Many of your goals may improve you by default as to progress in achieving their fulfilment, but you must also take into consideration directly taking time to upskill you.

Upskilling yourself means taking time to read, learn, and practice in areas that are suited to you that will help you become an improved person. This will also help you to increase the likelihood of achieving any goals you set for your life. What could you read right now that could make a difference in your life? Is there something you can practice to refine your skill set in a particular area? What could you learn right now that could sharpen your skill set and knowledge base?

One of the biggest investments you will ever make will be in yourself. Each and every time you decide to improve who you are in some way or another, you will benefit greatly in many ways. Every time you learn something new, gain a new perspective, or perfect your skills through practise, you always open yourself up to manifest new opportunities in the future. All self-improvement leads you forward constructively. The more you learn, the more knowledge you possess, the sharper your skills, the more valuable you are to other people and organisations who know how to take your skills and leverage them.

"One of the biggest investments you will ever make will be in yourself.

No matter what is happening in your life at any point in time, how to leverage your time to your advantage will very much determine how much you achieve in life and how successful you become. There is no better time than a crisis to decide to dig in your heals and leverage your time to your advantage, so you come out the other side better than ever. Don't let fear, worry, doubt, and uncertainty stop you right now. Always ask yourself, what can I do right now which will make the biggest difference in my life?

Any time you make the effort to upskill yourself, you will always benefit. Opportunity is everything. If you can leverage yourself to be in a position where you manifest more opportunity for yourself regularly, the direction your life takes will surprise you.

With each new opportunity comes another possibility which, if maximised, can dramatically change the direction of your life for the better.

There is no downside to an improved mind. Each time you make the effort to improve yourself, you will be rewarded. You give yourself an advantage over others every time you upskill your intellectual understanding. The world is becoming increasingly competitive more than ever before. Wouldn't you like to have the advantage? Gain as much knowledge as you can? It will give you the edge over your competition. Take the time now to prepare yourself for the person you want to be in the future. Time passes quickly. Before you know it, a month will have passed. Looking back, will it have been a productive time in your life? Or did you ignore what was within your power to control?

Build on Your Relationships

YOUR ABILITY TO fulfil your social needs may be reduced significantly as you endure this time of crisis. You may lack motivation and want to isolate yourself from others. A lack in social interaction will have a tremendous impact on your mental health. Often, we overlook the importance of having access to other people and our freedom to socialise. But without social interaction, your psychological well-being will deteriorate rapidly.

Despite the motivation to socialise for the sake of our health, there are still many really meaningful benefits in interacting with people beyond our conscious awareness. Now, more than ever, you need people. There's no real excuse for not making the effort. Maximise your time by making the effort to build on your relationships in hard times. You can always pick up the phone to stay in touch with your colleagues. You can FaceTime or Skype with family members. You can even take the time to email a friend.

Use your time to check in with those you care about. Don't wait for them to reach out. Accept the responsibility to initiate communications. Have you considered that there may be people out there struggling with their own mental health? By making the effort to check in on another person, you can make them feel important and valued. It could make all the difference in a person's life. It can provide you and the other person with the opportunity to focus on something other than problems. It can be quite invaluable.

Take the time to contact those people you suspect may need some encouragement. Check in on them. If you're aware that a person might be struggling--reach out. Most people tend to struggle with isolation in hard times if they are left all alone. One phone call, every now and again, can be enough to prevent you and another person from experiencing depression. Don't under-estimate the power you have in using your words to encourage others. People never go backwards when positively encouraged. Knowing you have made a difference in another person's life can be extremely valuable to your own mental health.

Use your time to check in with those you care about.

We all have a responsibility to look out for, and provide for, the most vulnerable when a crisis hits us. Be what other people need. If you make the effort to contribute to the quality of another person's well-being, it will produce levels of fulfilment within you which keep you in a good psychological state of being. Making a difference in another person's life is one of the best tonics for sound mental functioning. Keeping an eye open for the well-being of other people also allows you to focus on something constructive. It gives you a high level of purpose. It might me a good idea to add into your weekly plan who you might call and when. It may be a good idea each day to see if you can think of someone who may need some encouragement.

" Take the time to contact those people you suspect may need some encouragement.

Accept people as they are despite any of your past interactions with them. Sometimes we become hesitant in contacting particular people because of things not spoken and past hurts. Don't let fear and uncertainty stop you from making contact. Times of crisis cause many people to let go of some of the silly things they were holding onto in favour of things which now seem much more important. Make the effort to make contact. It will be good for you.

Plan for the Future Now

TAKE THIS TIME to strategize potential outcomes for your future now. While none of us can truly predict the future, and many external things are beyond our direct control, it is good to take time to develop a plan of action in the present. Rather than feeling helpless right now, take time to strategize different potential outcomes and possibilities. Having a plan allows you to prepare your resources in advance. Having a plan gives you a sense of control, even though everything else seems to be out of control.

"Take this time to strategize potential outcomes for your future now.

Rather than thinking about future events in negative disempowering ways that lead to fear, worry, doubt, and uncertainty, channel your focus forward constructively. Think forward in ways that serve your psychological well-being to your advantage. It would be wise to execute anything you can do right now in the present moment in order to enhance your chances of future success. Take some time out to reflect upon, plan, and strategise what your future life looks like now, because this crisis won't last forever.

Don't overdo it. I wouldn't recommend spending a great deal of your time regularly pondering your future. And if you don't have all the answers right now, that is okay. You're not meant to have all the answers right now in advance. Strategizing now is more about knowing how you might react to future events if they were to happen so you have a plan. Being able to anticipate possibilities of what could or might happen can be constructive and healthy. If, however, you observe any negative psychological patterns that are disempowering, take some time out emotionally. Don't try to look forward if you are struggling to cope in the moment.

" Despite the temptation of negative perception, this time in your life can be fruitful in many different ways if you allow it.

Despite the temptation of negative perception, this time in your life can be fruitful in many different ways if you allow it. Can you get out of your own way? Can you bypass fear and uncertainty in favour of accepting responsibility for what you can control? There is no rule in your life that determines whether or not this time is productive and advantageous. What you believe will ultimately determine your immediate experience. The manifestation of a crisis does not mean you are bound and powerless. You can still flourish and thrive right now despite how things appear on the outside.

With many of your freedoms being stripped from you, be more determined than ever to make sure you come out the other side better than ever. Passionately execute whatever it is that you need to manifest in order to make this time productive and beneficial to you in the future. Make sure you do everything within your power right now, so you set yourself up to win in the future. Take this present time to do what other people won't. Their refusal to do what needs to be done to ensure a bright future is to your advantage. Anything you do that another person does not will position you above your competition.

Start planning for the future now. You are in control. Design your life the way you want it to be. You realise you have the power to design your own life, right? You don't have to react to what others expect of you. Your life is yours to direct in any way you choose. Choose well. You only get to live it once.

PART 2

Psychological Self-Care

There's No Right or Wrong Way To Get Through a Crisis

THERE IS ONE important point that we must accept when we find ourselves enduring a crisis. We must simply accept there's no right or wrong way to navigate through a crisis. You must allow yourself to find the best way forward while minimising your own personal expectations. Any expectations you have right now regarding how things should be, how you should be, what you should be doing, etc., will only result in you feeling pressured. The last thing you need right now is self-imposed pressure because you're being hard on yourself.

Much of the time, when external events are beyond our control, we have to adjust and adapt constantly to what we are experiencing moment by moment. You won't always know what to do or how to do it. You won't always react rationally by default. But that's okay. In a time of crisis, it's important for you to be kind to yourself. Accepting yourself as you are right now is an important psychological tool that will allow you to keep moving forward with momentum despite expectation.

When we lack the intellectual understanding needed to maintain psychological control, it can be very difficult to stay calm without reacting with a negative emotional response by default. Again, there is no right or wrong way to respond to more bad news or new challenges which come to your attention. Obviously, there is an ideal pathway which would be best to take in order to maintain good psychological and emotion well-being. But sometimes in a crisis, with so much built up pressure, it can be extremely hard not to explode.

> "We must simply accept there's no right or wrong way to navigate through a crisis.

We must let go of the idea of right and wrong as we attempt to move forward. What happens if you perceive something you've done to be wrong? Won't you beat yourself up for it? Most will in some way. And, if things have to go right for you in order for you to be happy, when will they go right? What happens if they don't go right? Will you be miserable until you get what you want? Again, most will. In times of crisis, sometimes all we can do is accept ourselves as we are and move forward to the best of our ability moment by moment. This is all you can really expect from yourself.

Having a routine, a plan for the week, and a plan for each day, while so advantageous to your psychological and emotional well-being, must still allow for some flexibility. You need to indulge in a moment of weakness every now and again. Even a psychological meltdown that has you reaching for the chocolate is okay. There is no right or wrong way. Give yourself permission to have a few moments of weakness. Just make sure that if you do have a moment of weakness, or if you find yourself experiencing a temporary meltdown, that you move on quickly. It's acceptable to release some pressure every now and again, even though others might perceive this to be a negative reaction. Just don't wallow in anger, misery, sadness, and frustration for too long. Eventually you need to make the decision to do what you know must be done to regain psychological control and emotional stability. Survival is about *surviving.* Sometimes surviving isn't pretty. It's okay to feel lost. Do whatever you need to do in order to survive this day the best way you can.

You Don't Have to Have All the Answers Right Now

IT'S OKAY TO feel lost. Give yourself permission to not know all the answers right now. There are so many things beyond your direct control. Trying to control what you don't really have control over will only lead to the experience of psychological torment and emotional trauma. Not knowing how things might work out is okay; but trying to control things you have no control over is not. In crisis you must control what is yours to control. You can control what you think, what you choose to believe, and how you react. Focus your energy onto what's yours to control, and you will find yourself escaping the torment and trauma associated with your attempts to control things that are beyond your ability to control.

It is quite normal to worry about what could happen or how things might work out during hard times. But you don't want to indulge in worrying for too long. If you do, you're at risk of manifesting the type of experience which forces your brain to believe what you're worrying about. If you believe what you have previously worried about, that belief will force a behavioural change in you. This is why it's best to regain psychological control of yourself as soon as you can whenever you notice any negative thought processes attempting to overwhelm you.

Your psychological and emotional well-being will suffer if you need to know all the answers and outcomes right away by trying to predict future events before they occur. If your focus is set all day on trying to predict future outcomes, you are torturing yourself. You are actively working toward your own ruin. What you think is yours to control, remember? You must take control of your focus and channel your thoughts into whatever serves you better, producing the good emotions you desire to experience.

Nothing you do right now will help you predict what's going to happen or when. You will suffer if you continually let yourself visualise potential possibilities in the future. Visualising future outcomes is nothing more than imagination in overdrive. The negative use of imagination in overdrive always leads to a person's psychological self-destruction. This is something within your control. For the sake of your own mental health, you must take control.

Plan for the future and strategise what could happen, and how you might need to react to particular situations; but accept that you can't predict the future. Don't even try. Accept you won't have all the answers in advance right now.

Focus on today. Don't try to look too far ahead. Keep your focus on the present moment and your immediate future. The answers you desire will come to you eventually. As each day passes without knowing, that brings you a day closer to finally having the answers you desire. The only certainty you need right now is found in knowing that, no matter what happens, you are strong enough to deal with it. And no matter what happens, you know you have what it takes to do what needs to be done, so you can come out on the other side better than ever. *Believe* it.

Live in the Present Moment

YOUR BEST CHANCE of escaping any past event that haunts you, or any fear, worry, doubt or uncertainty is to focus your mind on the present moment. Your imagination is simply in overdrive. Is the past happening in the present moment? No. Is the future happening in the present moment? No. Only this moment exists. When your mind is focused on the present moment, you escape all the torment and trauma associated with future and past events.

The only way the past can hurt you right now, in this present moment, is if you make the conscious decision to think about it; therefore, you're bringing the past in to the present. *You* did this. The future can't hurt you right now; it hasn't happened. But, if you let your imagination run in overdrive, guess what you'll experience? All the fear-based emotions you really don't want will only stimulate your overthinking and become even more rapid right now.

Live in the present moment. The present moment is your escape. Psychological calm is found in the present moment only. Emotional stability comes about only when we focus on the here and now. There is nothing more important than living in the present moment, moment by moment. All of your pain, all the psychological torment you have ever experienced, all the terrible emotions you've experienced, have always been the result of living in the past or in the future in the present moment. Think about it. Is this not true?

" *The present moment is your escape.*

Remember this: any future psychological pain you experience that results in unwanted emotions will be due to you channelling your intellectual focus on either past or future events in some way. How you channel your attention is within your control. Keep your attention on right here, right now. Let your focus be on what is happening within this moment only. Then you will experience the emotional freedom you desire with the clarity of mind you deserve.

Leverage your capacity to ignore the past. It's done now, and you can't change it. Leverage ignorance to your advantage by ignoring potential future possibilities. Don't look too far ahead. Keep striving to be your best right here, right now. Focus on what you need to do right now only. Ignorance will be your best friend if you use it to your advantage. Leveraging ignorance to your advantage is a skill worth developing. It will serve you powerfully.

The quality of your life really is determined by the quality of your psychological states and emotional experiences throughout your journey. What quality of life have you been experiencing? Has fear been worth it? Has your replaying of past events been worth it? Is a mind out of control really serving you to your advantage? Each moment you have an opportunity to design your life the way you want it to be by channelling your focus in the most advantageous way possible for you. Will you do it? Is it worth it? The quality of your life depends on it. Your mental health is not something worth ignoring. Live in the present moment as much as you can. This present moment is a gift. Use it to your advantage.

Take Responsibility for Controlling What You Can

IN A TIME of crisis, your main responsibility is managing what is happening within your own internal experience. The best way to address all the challenges you are facing is to withdraw from external influences by taking control of your internal experiences. Taking responsibility for what you can control is your best form of defence and attack when hard times hit. There is no higher responsibility than controlling what is happening within your own psychological and emotional experience.

> *Taking responsibility for what you can control is your best form of defence and attack when hard times hit.*

Navigating through a crisis well will require you to accept that you, and only you, are in control of what happens within your own psychological and emotional experiences. What you think is your responsibility. What you speak, and the words you absorb from other people, are yours to manage. What you see as being possible, and how you use your imagination, is your exclusive responsibility. You must accept your role in taking control for these things which are yours to control, or you will not cope. Maintaining good mental health while enduring though a crisis requires your participation.

Only you can channel your own thoughts and choose what to focus on. You, and only you, can do this within your internal experience. Yes, external things can happen that stimulate and influence you but, ultimately, is it not true that what happens within you is your choice? You decide what meaning you will give the events you have experienced. You determine what you will believe. Only you have this right. I don't; no one else does; just you.

So, rather than continuing to indulge in what has happened or why, or what might happen and when, why not cease entertaining these thoughts and live in the present moment?

Make the decision to control what happens within you. Determine for yourself the meaning behind what you experience. Decide to influence your own emotions to your advantage by controlling your intellectual focus right now. This has always been within your control. You may have suffered through many past events due to your inability to take control over your internal experience. Maybe you didn't even realise you could have control over what happens within you. Now you do know. So, do what you know must be done in order to experience the state of mind and emotional well-being you deserve right now in this moment.

Ask yourself: what could I think about right now that would allow me to feel empowered? How do I need to see myself right now that will inspire and motivate me? What do I need to keep saying to myself in order to maintain psychological balance right now? Answer these questions well, and you will become your own remedy. What you've needed to function to the best of your ability has always been within you. Now that you're starting to realise what's possible, do what you now know. Don't wait for another answer; be the answer you need right now. You won't regret taking control.

Control Your Focus

IN ORDER TO live in the present moment and take responsibility for what you can control right now, you must control your intellectual focus exclusively Your intellectual focus consists of thoughts, words (spoken and spoken to you), and vision (visualisation/imagination). How you manage your intellectual focus will determine directly your psychological state, as well as what range of emotions you are experiencing in the present moment.

Your intellectual focus can bring you full circle from starting point to end point in your immediate internal experience. Often, we overlook the power of what we think, what we say, what's being said to us, what we visualise, and what we imagine. Because we experience these things on a continual basis, we often diminish their importance in influencing our immediate experience. What is familiar very often loses our attention. When we pay no attention to the elements of our intellectual focus, we can soon find ourselves experiencing all kinds of negative psychological processes that can propel us into a range of negative, undesired emotions.

When you accept personal responsibility for controlling your own thoughts, what you say, the meaning of what's being said to you, what you visualise, and how you use your imagination, you will be rewarded with the most advantageous skill set you could ever acquire. When you master your intellectual focus with intention, it puts you in the ultimate state of personal control. The moment you accept this, you will transition from someone who reacts to the world around you, allowing it to manipulate your feelings, to someone who is grounded and empowered despite external circumstances.

Only you get to decide what you will think about. *You* get to decide how you will think about all things that you experience. Who you are and what you're capable of are your own choices. Whatever you choose to say becomes what you believe is possible. How you choose to see yourself is your right. You can be whoever you create yourself to be. Who do you want to be? What do you want to achieve? Who do you want to become? What do you want for your life? All of these things are yours to control by directing your intellectual focus down pathways that serve you best.

" Only you get to decide what you will think about.

What impacts you, what you absorb mentally from your experiences, are all yours to control. Just because an external event happened that was unexpected and undesired does not mean you have to buy into fear, worry, doubt, and uncertainty as your first, immediate reactions. *You* get to decide what you will experience based on all external events. External events don't have to impact you psychologically and emotionally before you choose to regain control. You can have control over external events immediately by choosing to direct your intellectual focus in the present moment in the most advantageous way to you. The meaning you associate to whatever is happening to you is yours, and only yours to control. Don't give the power to determine what you experience psychologically and emotionally over to the very things that have happened to you. Take back your responsibility to influence your own life, and never give this power to control your internal experience to anyone or anything ever again.

Be the Observer of Your Internal Experiences

IN CHOOSING TO take responsibility for what you can control in the present moment, and then directing your intellectual focus to your advantage, you must maintain a constant state of observation over all your internal processes. Moment by moment, you have a responsibility to observe your internal psychological and emotional experiences. We must be constantly evaluating what is happening within our internal experience and why. And then, through observing what we are experiencing, we must make the decision to execute our power and control over what we are experiencing. This will ensure that we experience the kind of psychological and emotional states we desire.

To observe our internal experience is to pay attention to *what* we are experiencing.

Once we are aware of what we are experiencing, then we must question the validity of our experience. Questions are a very powerful tool we can use to re-evaluate our internal experience. Simple questions such as: Why am I thinking this way? What influenced this cycle of thought? Why am I seeing things this way? Why do I believe this? These are just a few questions which can really help you diagnose the quality of your internal experience. As soon as you ask yourself a question, your brain goes to work to seek an answer. By indulging this type of questioning, you allow yourself to acknowledge anything which doesn't serve you and to take back control over it.

It is fully within your control to pay attention to what you experience and then question the authenticity of that experience. Most people will travel through life paying no attention to what is happening within them or why. They never seek answers, because they never question their experience. Living like this often leads to anxiety and depression. Your best defence in avoiding the consequences of anxiety and depression is to take control of what you can control. Observe what you are experiencing, question why you're experiencing it, and then take back control over your experience.

As you develop your ability to observe your internal experience, you may find that many of your habitual thought processes really don't serve you well at all. This is quite normal. As soon as we choose to observe our internal experience, we are opening our eyes up to things previously ignored. Each time we break down the barriers of our own ignorance, there is always a range of things we will discover and learn. Many of the things we discover in our observation of ourselves can be quite confronting at first.

" Observe what you are experiencing, question why you're experiencing it, and then take back control over your experience.

It may be intimidating to discover you were ignorant of things. But the lessons your observations provide to you are invaluable. You can't fix something when you don't know what the problem is, right? So, in becoming consciously aware through your own observation, you actually allow yourself to make corrections that will ultimately serve you if you choose to correct them. Maintain a conscious state of observation in each moment to the best of your ability. Continue developing your ability to observe. It will serve you well. Don't fear what you may discover. Pay attention and eliminate anything that does not serve you, so you can experience the quality of life you truly deserve.

Conscious Willingness

VOLITION IS ONE of the most significant tools we can apply in a time of crisis. Its application will enable us to transition forward empowered. Volition is simply conscious willingness. We must do what we know we must do. Each time we choose to consciously and willingly do what needs to be done in the present moment, we allow ourselves to move forward productively. Volition is the key. The difference between those who do and those who do not is volition. Those who keep moving forward are separated from those who remain stuck, miserable, and tormented by volition.

" Each time we choose to consciously and willingly do what needs to be done in the present moment, we allow ourselves to move forward productively.

The moment you make a conscious decision to accept responsibility for what you can do, then take action to control and you will benefit greatly. Your conscious willingness to take responsibility, and to do what has to be done, allows you to be the remedy to your own problems in many ways. What could you do if you were consciously willing? What could you achieve if you were consciously willing? What would the quality of your life be if you were consciously willing to do what needs to be done? In times of crisis, most people feel powerless, which leaves them feeling helpless. Volition gives you back control. Being consciously willing to do what needs to be done brings back confidence through empowerment.

Those who experience external events, and then suffer through the psychological torment and emotional trauma of a mind out of control, are simply ignorant to their power in controlling what is theirs to control. If you made the decision to read this book through from the start, you already possess enough intellectual understanding to regain control over your internal psychological and emotional experience. The only questions remaining are: will you now do what you know you must do? Will you now apply what you have learned? If you exert your power, your conscious willingness will reposition you to your advantage.

As always, the choice is yours. Volition puts you back in control. Conscious willingness to do what needs to be done makes you the master of your own destiny. How you navigate this time in your life is yours to control. You get to decide. You have the authority. You are the only power who has any control. To believe otherwise is to give in to delusion. If you make the conscious decision to turn your back on volition, you will continue through your stormy life as a rudderless ship. Without a rudder you cannot have control, the direction you head in will be left to chance, how you react will be autonomous, and you will be vulnerable to everything which happens around you. Your psychological state of being will be one of reaction rather than control. Your emotions will torment and traumatise you endlessly until you gain the courage to take back what is yours to control.

" Volition puts you back in control.

Your biggest advantage in life will be making the decision to continually execute your conscious willingness over time as you progress through your life. The more you get yourself to react by doing all the right things in your hardest times, the more you empower yourself to deal with all that life throws at you boldly over time. The more you execute your power through volition, the more you will come to realise that many things you face as you move forward are fully within your power to overcome and control. Volition will empower you to flourish and thrive in life despite whatever may be happening around you and to you.

Take Charge of Your Belief System

WHAT WE CHOOSE to believe is very often in reaction to our experiences. Often what we believe happens autonomously beyond our conscious awareness. Without making the conscious effort to observe our internal experience, in times of crisis we run the risk of what we are experiencing having the power to determine what we think, feel, and ultimately believe. To live life without conscious awareness of what we are believing and why is extremely dangerous and leaves us vulnerable to ourselves.

What we believe is the catalyst for how we behave. Your decisions are based on what you believe. So are your actions. You don't just blindly decide to do something. You do what aligns with what you believe. Navigating through a crisis of any kind successfully demands that you are the influencer of your own belief system. By default, as we grow and proceed to journey through our lives, we are often unequipped with the kind of beliefs that serve us. If we don't find a way to develop what we are believing, we will get stuck in the same behaviour patterns over time. We may long to change and grow but, until we change what we believe behaviourally, we will remain the same.

Your belief system is your own to control. To date, what you believe has been the result of your past experiences and the meaning you have associated to those past events. Belief is nothing more than a previously installed memory. These memories become the rulebook of our existence. And until we break down the beliefs which don't serve us and install what does, we will live life stuck and tormented by our own internal experience. In crisis, we must accept responsibility for controlling what we can. You can control what you decide to believe right now. The meaning you associate to any experience past, present, or future is yours to define right now. What you choose to believe right now will determine the quality of your immediate internal experience.

What has happened to you does not have control over you. What you believe based on your experience does have control. Another person does not have control over you, though they will if you don't take back control of your own internal experience right now. Nothing that has happened to you has any power over you. What you choose to believe to be true for you in this present, immediate moment is the only thing that matters. What you choose to believe right now is what defines who you are, what you're capable of, and what's possible.

Your true identity is not found in what you have or who likes you. Your true identity is defined only by what you choose to believe about you right now. If you have been beating yourself up over past events, what have you been believing that has caused you to behave this way? Have you been believing you're a failure, or not good enough? If you've given in to fear and uncertainty, what have you been believing? That it's not going to work out? Observe your behaviour and question what you have been believing that might be causing this behaviour. And then decide to believe something of your own choosing that enables and empowers you to move forward and experience the kind of psychological and emotional experience you desire most. In taking control of what you're choosing to believe right now, you are taking control of the greatest power you will ever have throughout your lifetime.

"*What you choose to believe right now is what defines who you are, what you're capable of, and what's possible.*

Beware of the Meaning
You Associate

MEANING IS POWERFUL. We apply it constantly throughout each moment of our existence. Rarely do we pay it any attention. Scarcely do we take control of it. The meaning we associate to what we are experiencing right now is critically important. Meaning is the catalyst even of what we choose to believe. If we aren't in control of the meaning we associate to our experiences, we are not in control of our lives. Everything you believe includes meaning. All your past experiences have had meaning associated to them. All your future based beliefs also have meaning associated to them.

Everything you experience right now, even reading this book, has your intellectual focus stimulated to the point where your brain has to interpret the stimulus and decide what it means. What it means will be associated by default, if you don't exert your power over being in conscious control of it. By default, meaning is actively being applied to your experiences right now. Every moment this is happening to you. Can you see how you might lose psychological control if you are not influencing the meaning you associate to your experiences?

Your experience of your life right now is a reaction to the meaning you have associated to all your experiences to date. The meaning you knowingly or unknowingly associate to everything within your experience is defining the quality of your experience right here, right now. Are you struggling to cope while you endure this time of crisis in your life? Well, what meaning have you been applying to your recent experiences? Is this meaning serving you right now? Or is it crushing you?

The way you define what has happened, what is happening, and what might happen, is your own personal choice. There is no greater responsibility than taking control of meaning. Be cautious of all your experiences as you experience them. Apply volition and make decisions willingly and consciously. Decide for yourself what your experience means and what you then choose to believe based on your experience. If you find yourself experiencing an unwanted psychological state of being as you endure this time in your life, take back control by choosing to redefine what your experiences mean.

You can influence what is or isn't possible in your life right now. How you move forward is yours to control. But you must choose to accept responsibility by executing what's yours to control.

Your past will determine what's possible for your future if you choose to ignore your power to take control. What's actually possible for you is open-ended and infinite. The possibilities you activate and give birth to in your life will be based on what you choose to believe right now in the present.

"There is no greater responsibility than taking control of meaning.

Meaning is everything. It has more of an effect on you that the event you experience or the person who hurt you. Yes, you may have been treated poorly. Yes, what happened to you may have been unfair. But no one and nothing that has happened to you were responsible for defining the meaning you proceeded to associate to your experience in that moment. You can't move forward successfully when you are blaming other people and other things that have happened to you as being responsible for your internal experience. Your internal experience is yours. Only yours. Take control of it. Redefine the meaning of all past events right now. Empower yourself once again by choosing to take control of what's always been exclusively yours to control.

Let Go of Expectation

WE NEED TO be wary of expectation when navigating our way forward in a time of crisis. Expectation can have a huge impact on our psychological well-being, influencing our emotions deceptively without our conscious awareness. Pre-crisis, our normal daily and weekly routines very much consist of the same cycle with the occasional variation. As we progress through each day and each week, we know mostly what to expect and can anticipate most things that will happen. This provides us a level of comfort.

We all have an unseen but very real and present internal map which tells us what we should expect and how life should be. Our map of how life should be is the rulebook we use to experience and play life. Our internal map, or rule book, is the accumulation of our expectations. Expectations are beliefs. For example, some of our personal expectations may include what we believe about how life is supposed to be, what should be happening right now, what we should do, what others should do, and how we must be treated.

If you want to progress forward well, despite all the challenges you are facing as you endure this hard time, you must pay attention to your own expectations. Unmet expectations can ruin you. If you have a rule that you live by that demands something in particular must happen as and when you need it to happen, or someone must say and do what you expect them to, what happens when your expectations aren't met? Will you cope? Will your internal experience be one of anger, frustrations, or sadness?

As you navigate through your time of crisis, it will be critical to your own mental health that you stop expecting anything to go the way you believed it should pre-crisis. In time of crisis, your old rule book no longer applies. A time of crisis is not your normal life. Crisis requires you to play life with a new rule book, one that is very much defined by circumstances and situations beyond your control. Your old rule book may have included expectations about how your external world should be, and how others should treat you. But when in a crisis, you must withdraw and take refuge in your internal world. You can no longer try to define your external world, because you have no real control over it all the time. But you do have control over your internal experiences.

In times of crisis we need to let go of our old external expectations and focus on our own internal expectations. Because we can only really control what happens inside of ourselves, we must choose to redefine our own expectations in order to set ourselves up to win. We must be flexible enough to let go of the frustration, anger, and sadness which manifest as the result of previously unmet expectations. We need to adapt to the external and internal environments we are now experiencing in this present moment in our time of crisis.

"In times of crisis we need to let go of our old external expectations and focus on our own internal expectations.

As you endure forward, if you don't harness your power to willingly redefine your expectations, you will suffer psychologically and emotionally. You risk manifesting anxiety and depression as your mind remains occupied with negative thought processes due to your expectations not being met. In times of uncertainty, it's best not to expect anything in your internal world to be or react as you expect. Accept that your map of how the world should be has temporarily been turned upside down. Don't let it ruin you psychologically. Take responsibility for controlling what is yours to control.

You Are Potential

RATHER THAN DWELLING on whether you have been mistreated by someone or are a victim of unfair recent events, instead focus upon the truth of who you are and on your capabilities. You are not defined by what has happened to you or how someone treated you. You are defined by nothing more than what you choose to believe to be true for you right now in this present moment. In this present moment, you must acknowledge and accept that you are *potential*.

You are *potential* as an intellectually thinking being capable of making decisions and taking action. In your time of crisis, you must accept that you are potential. As a being of potential, how you think, the decisions you make, and the actions you take right now will determine what possibilities are available to you as you progress forward. This present moment is an opportunity. When potential meets opportunity, we manifest new possibility.

" When potential meets opportunity, we manifest new possibility.

Despite what has happened to you, and what is happening to you right now, you can be the one who makes a difference in your life. You are packed with infinite potential, because you yourself are potential. If you ignore your potential right now, you will suffer. You are the remedy you need right now. What you think, what you decide, and what you do will determine how well you progress forward. These will be the determining factors in how well you cope psychologically and emotionally.

Despite whatever you are facing, no matter how bad it may seem, there are no limitations on you and your capabilities. *You* define you, not what has happened to you, not what other people think about you. You are a limitless form of potential. To allow your potential to manifest, you must accept that you are potential. How your life progresses, what you achieve, and how quickly you transition from this crisis to the next stage of your life will be decided by how well you allow yourself to take the opportunity you have to manifest new possibilities in this present moment.

You are not powerless. You have never truly been powerless despite the deception of your own thinking. Don't allow anyone or anything permission to have the power to determine who you are and what you're capable of. The right to determine you who you are and what you're capable of is yours exclusively. It's not up for negotiation. Stop giving the power to determine your identity over to people and circumstance. You are not who people say you are; you are who *you* say you are. You are not what has happened to you; you are what you choose to believe you are despite what's happened to you.

" *There is no external force that has any real power over you.*

There is no external force that has any real power over you. What you can do is determined only by you, by what you choose to think, the decisions you are courageous enough to make, and the actions you are bold enough to take. You've been deceived into believing you had no power and control. You *are* power and control, because you yourself are potential. No one can ever rob you of being potential. What do you want for your life? How do you want to move forward? Reflect, decide, act. You are in full control. The results you experience in the future will very much be decided by your conscious willingness to do what needs to be done.

What's Possible is Infinite

THERE ARE NO limits to what you can do, what you can become, and what you can achieve. What's possible for you is infinite. For many, this is extremely hard to acknowledge initially. After all, so far in your experience of life you've been conditioned to believe that what was possible for your life is based on the beliefs of other people around you. What your parents believed to be possible. How your friends and other people defined what's possible for you. And to this point, many of your experiences in life have defined your own perception of what you now believe to be possible. This includes all those times you perceived yourself failing in the past.

"There are no limits to what you can do, what you can become, and what you can achieve.

There are no limits to what is possible for you. Open your mind to a new possibility. Step away from your past conditioning. Distance yourself from your old programming so you can entertain a new possibility. There is no limit to what is possible for you. I get it, life may have been cruel, you've been beaten by life over and over again, but you're still standing. You're still very much in the game. What you've been through, and all you've overcome so far in life, reveal the real truth of who you are and what you're capable of. To endure all you've been through and still be here looking to move forward reveals you are a person of real strength. Despite the current crisis you are enduring, you are still enduring. This demonstrates real character.

Entertaining the idea of new future possibilities is exciting. As you entertain new possibilities, you get to be the architect of your own life. This can be a tremendously liberating experience. Realising your own personal power in being the creator of your own future life gives you back a sense of power and control. There is no limit to what you see for yourself. There are no limits to what you decide and what action you allow yourself to take. Stepping away from the apparent limitations of your immediate experience while in crisis, and entertaining future experiences of your own creation, is a powerful way to set yourself up to flourish and thrive despite what you are facing right now.

Have fun with possibility. If you choose to do so, you get to reinvent yourself many times over throughout your lifetime. Reach into the realm of the unknown. Bring to life what you see. Action it now in this present moment. Make some decisions now that will move you toward obtaining the possibility you have seen. Don't allow this current situation to define you. Define yourself. Looking forward and entertaining new possibilities for your life is a form of escape. Entertaining new possibilities puts your imagination to work in a positive way.

" *Dreams are fantasy. Possibilities are potential realities. Don't dream: believe in your potential to manifest possibilities into reality.*

Believe you can have what you see. Any possibility is possible. The moment you identify a possibility that appeals to you, believe you can have it. Even if you don't yet know how to manifest what you see right now, never stop believing in the possibility you have seen for your life. Your responsibility is not to know every detail about how, when, and what will manifest into your reality. Your responsibility is to believe you can have what you can see. You must believe it is yours in advance of receiving it. Dreams are fantasy. Possibilities are potential realities. Don't dream: believe in your potential to manifest possibilities into reality. Your life is not some fantasy. It is very much an experience of reality influenced by potential manifesting possibility into its reality.

Possibility is Based on Belief

THE MANIFESTATION OF possibility into your reality will require you to form a new set of beliefs that support the manifestation of your possibility. To see something as being possible is not enough: we have to believe in it. To believe in it once, and then dismiss it moving forward, will not allow possibility to manifest. You have a responsibility to continually move towards what you perceived to be possible. There must be a persistent determination to do whatever it takes to manifest your possibility into your reality. You can't just leave what's possible up to the universe without no effort on your part.

" To see something as being possible is not enough: we have to believe in it.

What's possible is infinite, but what you believe will determine if your possibility becomes a reality. Thinking something is possible must be backed up by believing it's possible. Belief determines behaviour. If you want a new possibility to manifest in your experience, how must you behave? What must you believe in order to behave that way? The choice is yours. Is the new possibility you have seen worth it? Will you take responsibility for controlling what you can so you can give birth to what you have seen?

You are what you believe. You are not what you wear, what you have, what you have achieved, or what other people say about you. You are nothing more than what you choose to believe you are. There is no other determining factor in your life. What you believe is it. Will you believe what you need to in order to manifest a great quality of life for yourself? The choice is yours. What's possible is of your own making. You are the creator of the experience of your own life.

" Belief determines behaviour.

Being in a crisis does not mean life is over for you. A crisis is a short-term experience of life. It's not permanent. You must put your experience in perspective. In crisis, it can feel like you are going to have to endure this hard time forever, but that is nothing more than a lie. What other possibilities can you entertain right now so you can perceive a brighter future? How can you influence the quality of your immediate experience right now despite what you are facing? What must you believe to ensure your experience of life is as good as it can be right now?

When you take this opportunity to redefine what you believe right now in this present moment, you open the pathway of possibilities manifesting themselves in your immediate experience. Your life is too important to entertain anything that does not serve you psychologically. Fear, worry, doubt, frustration, and anger all manifest possibility in your immediate experience of reality. Do you really want what's possible for you in this lifetime to be defined by the type of negative emotions and corrupt thought processes you experience?

"Give new possibilities permission to make themselves present in your immediate experience by choosing to believe in them.

With each new empowering belief installed, you expand the previously defined limitations of your own personal possibilities. What you believe can drive you to manifest possibilities beyond what you ever thought to be possible in your life. As you execute your own personal power and control over what you believe you enable things you believe to be possible to manifest within your reality with complete authority. Give new possibilities permission to make themselves present in your immediate experience by choosing to believe in them.

The Present Moment is an Opportunity

THE SIGNIFICANCE OF the present moment is often overlooked. As we move forward with our lives, we usually live life looking back or looking forward while ignoring the moment we are actually experiencing. The present moment really is a gift. It provides us with endless opportunities. No matter what has happened to you, or what you have done in the past, right now you have a wonderful gift which is the key to a better future. If you accept willingly the gift which is the present moment, and take advantage of what you've received, you can transform your life.

Nothing can ever rob you of opportunity. It doesn't matter what has happened or where you find yourself right now, nothing and no one has any control over your internal psychological and emotional experience. Therefore, you will always find opportunity to be present in your life. The decisions you make right now, and the actions you take based on those decisions, are directly responsible for your destiny. Destiny is not some random happening; it's purposeful. Destiny is decided very much by you.

You're destined for greatness if you first believe in your own greatness. You have what it takes to create any life for yourself that you can imagine. Nothing can stop you from having what you believe is possible, if you are determined to ensure you will do everything within your power to manifest it. Whether or not you believe you're good enough to have it, and whether you believe you deserve it, are two areas you will need to enhance in your belief system in order to prevent conflict. If you want what you believe is possible but don't believe you deserve it, do you think it will happen? If you want something different but don't believe you are good enough to have it, do you think it will happen? It won't. You can't truly believe something to be a possibility for yourself if you don't believe you are good enough or deserve it in the first place.

" You're destined for greatness if you
first believe in your own greatness.

Rather than see yourself as inferior and inadequate, see yourself as a creator. You *are* a creator. Your capacity to create anything you desire in your life is exclusively within your control. When you take responsibility for yourself by controlling what is yours to control, you are executing your power to create. When you design your life the way you want it, you possess luxury in life. Don't settle for less than you deserve in life by choosing to conform to what other people and society dictate about your life.

Conformity kills possibility. You will never reach your highest potential if you continue in the same cycles of conformity as you have always done. To experience something new, you will have to expose yourself to things you've never done before.

You don't need anyone's permission to live the life you most desire. You are the only authority in your life who has control over your internal psychological and emotional experiences. You are responsible for governing what happens within you. You are the enforcer of your own psychological experience. You are the influencer of your own emotions. You get to be the surgeon of your own life; you get to remove any belief which doesn't serve you and replace it with something empowering. Accept your responsibility to control what is yours in the present moment. Be your own remedy.

PART 3

Emotional Self-Care

Thoughts Create Feelings

THOUGHTS ARE SUCH a constant experience within our internal experience that we often overlook their significance. In ignoring the significance of thoughts, we dismiss their power in influencing our lives. It is important that we give our thoughts the attention they deserve and acknowledge their power in influencing our immediate experience. Thoughts are the catalyst event; they are the cause before the effect of emotion. If we ignore the power of thought to influence our emotional experience, our immediate experience of emotion will be left to the processes happening beyond our conscious awareness.

"*Thoughts are the catalyst event; they are the cause before the effect of emotion.*

Ultimately, what you think is directly responsible for what you feel. Feelings don't just happen to you for no reason; they are the manifestation of your own creation. What you feel isn't just happening to you. What you think is the root cause of what you are feeling. With the exception of physical pain in the body influencing your emotions, no matter what situation you find yourself in right now, no matter what has happened to you or who hurt you, how you're processing the events you've experienced in the past is responsible for creating the emotions in your immediate experience, right now in this present moment.

Understanding thought to be the catalyst event which produces by default a chemical response in your brain will be critical for you to acknowledge as you move forward. If you attempt to navigate your way through your crisis, letting your thoughts run wild and out of control, having no direct influence over what is happening within your internal experience, you will suffer greatly. It can be hard to accept our own personal responsibility in creating the misery we are experiencing due to not taking responsibility for our own thought processes. But it was never what happened to you, or who hurt you, which truly hurt you; it was the meaning you associated to your experience which influenced you to think a certain way. Your thoughts have been impacted significantly by your inability to define proper meaning to your experiences.

You are in control of what you think; therefore, you are in control of what you feel. It will always be this way. Taking psychological responsibility for what happens in your own internal experience will by default influence you emotionally. Knowing thoughts create emotion, how can you influence your thought processes to your own advantage? What must you think? How must you direct your intellectual focus to your advantage so you can create the emotional experience you desire despite what you are experiencing?

Over time, as you develop your ability to influence your emotions through your own thought processes, the challenges you face in the future won't seem as big or dramatic. When you know that, no matter what, everything that happens in your external experience is defined by what happens within your internal experience, and then choose to apply what you know, life transforms. Accepting this responsibility gives you such an advantage in life. The more capacity you have to face whatever life throws at you while remaining calm and in control, navigating your way forward, you will find yourself being able to progress rapidly by achieving more than you believed to be possible.

Understanding Happiness

IN THE PURSUIT of a pleasurable life, we very much pursue happiness, hoping it will be the force that determines our quality of life. States of pleasure are the most enjoyable experiences we seek throughout our lifetimes. To obtain pleasure in life, there is no limit to what a person will use in an attempt to possess it. However, most people pursue happiness with no conscious awareness of what it is or why they are chasing it. So, let me ask you: what is happiness? Do you even know? I'm not asking what it would take for you to be happy, or what you need to be happy; I'm asking what is happiness itself?

It is critical to our own state of being that we understand what happiness is because, pursuing it blindly without even understanding what it is or why we are chasing it, can be one of the most destructive influencers over our entire lifetime. Here is the answer: happiness is nothing more than an emotional experience. Happiness itself is the manifestation of desired emotions. We only experience these desired emotions when our expectations are met as we expect them to be met. In other words, you are only happy, and you only experience the emotional experience of happiness, when you get what you want. When you don't get what you want, you are miserable.

" Happiness is nothing more than
an emotional experience.

In times of crisis, we are not getting what we want, and our expectations aren't being met as we desire. So then, how are we supposed to obtain happiness? It can't be possible. I want something, and I'm not getting it. I expect this, and I'm not getting it. How then are you supposed to be happy? Here is the problem with happiness: everyone chases happiness through external vehicles. The truth is, nothing and no one can truly meet your needs as you need them met all the time. So, what happens then if someone leaves you? What happens if you lose your job? How will you react if your happiness depended on your partner? How will you cope if you formed your identity around your career? Will you cope?

We are obsessed with obtaining the emotional experiences we desire most, using everything and anything we can find outside of ourselves, when the truth is real happiness is only ever found from within, and it's not called happiness. There is an emotional experience which surpasses happiness, and that is found in contentment and fulfilment. People often chase things externally in the hope of happiness so they can experience contentment and fulfilment; but it never works. Those external vehicles we use to gain happiness are variable subject to change. If they can change, that means they have the power to influence you negatively.

You are a constant variable. In your internal experience you can withdraw as a refuge. You can always achieve contentment and fulfilment in your internal experience if you choose to be in control of what happens in your psychological and emotional experience. A calm mind and emotional freedom create contentment and fulfilment. So, if you want to navigate your way through your crisis well, take control of your internal experience. Don't let external vehicles define whether or not you will be able to achieve happiness. Escape to the refuge of a calm mind and emotional stability by taking control of your internal experience. In this way, you can rise above the pettiness of seeking happiness through external events and other people. The quality of your emotional experience is defined by you; it is your responsibility.

The Power of Words

SINCE WE USE words constantly, it is easy to dismiss their power as we release them into our experience, at times recklessly, and being consciously unaware of their direct impact. Words have the power to trap us. Our psychological freedom very much depends on how we choose to use the words we speak. Words define us. What we speak influences what we believe. What we believe is directly responsible for creating our own personal identify.

"Words have the power to trap us.

When we do not pay attention to the words we speak, we can make tremendous mistakes in our lives. The words we choose to speak can keep us permanently entrapped in psychological darkness and unable to break free. You believe what you say. The more you continue to reinforce what you believe with your words, the harder it will be for you to entertain other possibilities.

Words themselves can be more influential than any external event we experience. Words go deep. It's not only the words we speak ourselves that can have an impact on our identity, but what other people speak greatly influences your self-perception as well. What defines who you are and what you're capable of? Words. What are beliefs made up of? Words. What is meaning? Words. Words impact every part of your psychological and emotional experience of life.

Without conscious awareness and living psychologically out of control, we are at risk of reacting to the words we process from both internal and external sources. We are unaware that the influence of words can soon have us feeling defeated and powerless. Words are the catalyst event and cause of helplessness. You do not have to be helpless during a time of crisis. You can direct your emotional experience by taking control of your psychological experience right now by being purposeful in your choice of words. Will you use them to build yourself up and empower yourself? Or will you use them in a way which leads to defeat and personal ruin?

Every word you speak and that has been spoken to you, including reading through this book, has the power to manipulate your belief system. Your belief system is your true identity. What you believe determines your behaviour; so it is essential to manipulate your own belief system back in your own favour. If you don't take control over the power of words in your life, you run the risk of every reckless word spoken by you and to you determining what you believe to be true for you by default without any conscious participation on your part. To live like this is dangerous.

At all times it is essential to observe the quality of the words you are speaking. Discern whether there is validity in speaking words into existence *before* you speak them. Assess if there is a chance that they will reinforce you negatively. Especially in a time of crisis, you cannot afford to contribute to your own disempowerment through the use of reckless words spoken carelessly. Pay attention and observe what you are speaking. Know that what you say directly influences who you are and what you're capable of in the most significant way.

You Create What You Think

THINKING IS THE root cause of all psychological and emotional pain. For the untrained, escaping negative, disempowering thought patterns seems to be impossible. Thinking is equally the starting point and the end point of all the internal pain you have ever experienced. Thought unharnessed is dangerous. Most people live their entire lifetime participating in thoughts without learning to tame them. Being able to directly influence your thought processes to your own advantage is an essential skill that must be developed within every single person.

Your chances of living a good life, whatever that may be for you, require some way to control your internal experience so you can then directly influence your path in the most advantageous way to you. Without the application of this skill, achieving the emotional states we desire most will not be possible on a regular basis. In order to give yourself the best chance of progressing through this time of crisis in good shape psychologically and emotionally, you will have to make the decision to consciously and willingly observe what is happening within your thought processes moment by moment.

To truly observe what is happening within your thought processes, you must pay attention by observing what you experience without any of your own personal judgement, conclusions, and prejudices. You have to remove yourself from your own personal wants and desires in order to observe what you are experiencing in an authentic manner. Since thoughts are the root cause of your unwanted psychological experience, they can only be truly observed when you detach your egocentric self from the process of observation.

"Thinking is the root cause of all psychological and emotional pain.

Your thoughts create your immediate experience. The five senses, what you think, what you see, what you say, and what you hear, all influence your own internal thought processes and determine how you feel in this present moment. Without the intellectual understanding needed to make sense of our internal experience, our thought processes become extremely dangerous. If we remain unaware, our thoughts can soon deceive us into all kinds of delusional beliefs based on the corruption of the thought processes.

When we live life not knowing how to influence and direct our thought processes, we succumb to the delusions manifested through our own deception. This is the cause of all the psychological torment and emotional trauma we experience. Thoughts have creative power; they can create joy, contentment, and fulfilment or misery. Thoughts themselves do not care about you. They will react, become, and do whatever they want to by default and autonomously without your permission if you ignore your power to control them.

"Your thoughts create your immediate experience.

If you do not apply what you know now, it will lead you into all sorts of delusional beliefs which do not serve you. It will make this experience you're in right now seem impossible to escape. Be vigilant; maintain a constant state of observation over your internal experience. Make the conscious decision to influence and direct thought to your advantage. You have the authority. Don't let out-of-control thought processes influence your perception. Actively participate in the creation of your own perception. What you think in this present moment is the catalyst which determines what you are experiencing emotionally right now. Choose well.

You Believe What You Can See

UNCONTROLLED THOUGHT PROCESSES automatically manifest imagery to support what you're thinking. Thought justifies itself by stimulating your internal visual senses with pictures congruent with what is being thought. To those who are visually orientated, they will experience the imagery of their thoughts before they are consciously aware that thought itself it the influencer of what has been seen. Visualisation through imagination can be one of our biggest enemies.

" Uncontrolled thought processes automatically manifest imagery to support what you're thinking.

When we lack intellectual understanding, by default what we see is what we believe. Once we see it, we entertain it. Because we can see it, we perceive there is justification in believing it. Without ever considering the validity of what we are seeing, many will accept and believe the narrative of their imagination without question. Imagination is powerful. Thought is the conductor of imagination. The limitation of thought leads to a limitation of imagination. If you can only see yourself one way, you shut yourself off from the possibility of seeing yourself any other way. Until you change what you think, you won't see anything different for yourself.

Your emotional experience is impacted directly through the imagery of thought. Like watching a movie, what you see impacts what you're thinking and feeling in that moment. So, thought leads to visual imagery, then visual imagery stimulates more thought, leading to even more visual imagery. The cycle is never-ending while you entertain it. This is why it can seem so hard to break out of your rut when you're out of control psychologically and emotionally.

"
Your emotional experience is impacted directly through the imagery of thought.

The major catalyst of thought is belief, which is nothing more than memory of the past experience stored. And both external and internal stimuli which provoke thought to search for meaning. If you do not actively participate in the installation of belief which serves you, you will find it difficult to maintain a state of calm and control without being reactionary when you experience challenges in life. If you don't like what you see, you can change it. Thinking differently will stimulate a different visual image. Use your imagination to create the imagery that empowers you best, and then believe what you see as possible.

If you can imagine it, you can have it. Rather than seeing yourself struggling and only just getting by, choose to see yourself as calm, in control, empowered, victorious. See yourself on the other side of your crisis now in advance. Don't let the picture go. As you create new imagery and choose to believe in what you see, you are having a direct impact on your belief system. Remember: you believe what you see. Just because you see it in your imagination does not mean it will happen by default. You still have to participate in taking the right action each day as you move forward. However, the psychological and emotional responses stimulated via thought processes of your own choosing will lead to empowerment rather than disempowerment. You will find yourself driven and determined rather than disconnected and disabled.

You are the creator of your own visual narrative. See all the possibilities available to you. There are no limits to what you can see. Choose to stimulate your thought processes to your advantage. Gravitate toward the good things you see. It will only feel like you're in a doom and gloom situation if you choose to see the visual imagery which supports that emotional response.

Belief Determines Behaviour

THOUGHTS, VISUAL IMAGERY, imagination, and emotion are all behaviours. They are behaviours of our internal experience with the power to determine our physical and external experiences. Belief is the catalyst event which precedes all thought, visual imagery, imagination, and emotion. If your experience of life right now does not meet your expectations, it is because you do not have a belief system which supports achieving and living the experience of life you desire.

Belief determines behaviour. Anxiety and depression are experiences manifested through belief. Our actions are determined by what we believe. If our immediate reaction creates an undesired psychological and emotional response, it was our belief system which caused the effect. Your internal experience does not just happen to you; it is very much a purposeful manifestation of belief directly stimulating thought that causes visual imagery and imagination to stimulate emotion. All your behaviour, whether purposeful or in reaction, has always been based exclusively on what you believed in that present moment.

This can be difficult to digest at first. The reason for this is because what we believe is stored consciously and subconsciously. Many of our deepest beliefs are stored beyond conscious access in our subconscious mind. If I were to ask you what you believe right now, subconsciously you wouldn't be able to tell me. You would give me an answer based on what you believe consciously right now in this moment, and it would not be an accurate response. The only way we can learn what someone believes subconsciously is through observing their behaviour. Behaviour reveals conscious and subconscious belief systems accurately.

"*Belief determines behaviour.*

Your behaviours are not a random manifestation. How you react, and what you do in response to the crisis you find yourself experiencing, are all determined by what you're believing in the moment. Your behaviour is intentional, even if reactionary. What you believe knowingly or unknowingly caused your reaction. If you find yourself in a psychological rut due to the crisis you're in, one belief you may need to develop is that creating the effort to do what is necessary is worth it.

You now have the reason for all your past reactions, and you now possess the answer which will allow you to create the quality of psychological and emotional experiences most beneficial to you despite the crisis. The only reason you couldn't change your behaviour previously is because you didn't realise its cause. Change what you believe now, and you are back in control. The only things worth believing in are those which enable and empower you to navigate this time in your life to the best of your ability, and those that allow you to reach your highest potential.

"Your behaviour is intentional, even if reactionary

You determine what you will believe. Empowering beliefs lead to empowering decisions. Empowering decisions lead to empowering actions. When you change what you believe, you change how you act by default. Any time you choose to believe in something which allows you to access a higher possibility for your life, you will gravitate automatically toward results that produce experiences beyond your expectations.

Psychological Control Manifests Emotional Calm

OUR BIGGEST DESIRE in life is to manifest within ourselves the kind of emotional experience we find most pleasurable. There's no limit to how we will delude ourselves in order to justify whatever it is we have found to gain the emotional experience we desire. Even if that means settling for less than we deserve. The emotional experience that serves us best is not found in external things such as what we have or who likes us. True pleasure is not found in the things we use to escape our unwanted emotional experience either. Drugs, alcohol, food, gambling, sex, or any other form of socially acceptable entertainment, will not give us what we really want.

The greatest emotional experience we can have is found only in contentment and fulfilment. True internal contentment and fulfilment bring peace, both psychological peace and emotional peace. Without psychological and emotional peace, we aren't really experiencing the emotional experience most beneficial to us. It is common for many people to travel through life in pursuit of happiness in one form or another without really knowing what true happiness is or where it comes from.

Happiness is not happiness without contentment and fulfilment in our internal experience. Psychological contentment leads to emotional fulfilment. The biggest tragedy of our lives is not knowing how to achieve psychological contentment and emotional fulfilment. Contentment and fulfilment are possible despite whatever is happening within your immediate experience. What may be stopping you from achieving it is first acknowledging that is possible and, second, not believing it to be possible.

When you take responsibility for controlling what is yours to control, you provide yourself an opportunity to create the emotional experience you desire despite anything you're facing right now. Nothing that has happened to you can determine what you experience psychically unless you let it. No one gets to determine what you experience emotionally. Only you do. Control your thoughts and create beliefs which support contentment and fulfilment right now, no matter what is happening around you.

Lack of intellectual understanding leads to a mind out of control. You now have all the intellectual understanding you will ever need. It is time for you to apply what you now know. In reading this book you now understand what is happening within you and why. The only thing stopping you from achieving psychological contentment and emotional fulfilment throughout this time in your life is your conscious willingness to action what you now know.

" Psychological contentment leads to emotional fulfilment.

Equipped with intellectual understanding, we can maintain a state of conscious awareness by choosing to take responsibility for what is ours to control. If your mind is in control, your emotions will be in control. You are your own responsibility now. Do what you know so you can escape the psychological torment and emotional trauma of your past experiences. Do so with consistency over time. Consistency over time equals permanent change. Keep doing what you know over and over again until you master your own power over controlling what is happening within your internal experience.

Also by Neil R. Oliver

About the Author

Neil R. Oliver is passionate about helping people escape the
psychological torment and emotional trauma of their experiences,
which many come to endure without intervention.

Please forward all enquires to info@neilroliver.com

www.neilroliver.com

CPSIA information can be obtained
at www.ICGtesting.com
Printed in the USA
BVHW091002130620
581406BV00012B/1175

9 780648 111368